1

Ultimate Dash Diet Cookbook

Enjoy a Healthier Lifestyle With Easy and Tasty Dash Diet Recipes

Brooke Weber

TABLE OF CONTENTS

INTRODUCTION

The DASH diet is designed to prevent the development of hypertension by changing the way we eat throughout our lives.

If you are unsure whether or not to follow a DASH diet plan, consult your doctor or dietician to determine which diet is best for you and your health, and what effect the diet has on your blood pressure. The dash diet is not the one that allows you to eat well for yourself, but rather for your health and well-being of the body. MD to assess your risk of heart disease, diabetes, high blood pressure and other health problems to determine the right diet plans.

A balanced diet that prevents high blood pressure by combining the DASH diet with exercise and weight control may be a better plan. While you can follow a low-calorie target plan on a dash diet, the focus will be on weight loss. If you want to lose weight with the "DASH diet," you probably need to go on a calorie-reducing diet. It can be difficult to see the difference in the effects of a strict diet compared to other diets when you try to lose weight with a DASH diet.

If you want to lower your blood pressure, improve your cardiovascular health and follow a nutritious diet to lose weight, experts praise the DASH diet as an effective way to help people improve their overall health. For this reason, we present the approach of stopping hypertension, which is praised for helping diabetics lose weight without side effects.

A subsequent study, known as "DASH and Sodium," assessed the effects of diet on blood pressure at different salt intake levels and showed that there was no difference in the effect of sodium when combined with the DASH diet. The researchers were able to determine the combined effect, and the results showed that there were no significant differences between the two diets in terms of their effects on blood pressure. However, the greatest reductions in blood pressure were achieved by eating a high-sodium diet, such as a high-sodium diet, a low-salt diet and a moderate to high-sodium diet. Both were successful in lowering blood pressure, but the benefits of a dash diet were greater when the salt intake was higher.

The DASH diet had the greatest effect in lowering blood pressure, while diets with additional fruits and vegetables showed interim results. In terms of weight loss, the dash diet alone was not as effective as another weight loss strategy - losing weight.

Researchers found that a high-fat version of the DASH diet lowered blood pressure without significantly increasing LDL cholesterol. The researchers agreed that the reasons for the decline in HDL levels need further investigation, but concluded that the dash diet overall is beneficial for heart disease.

To the best of our knowledge, this is the first study to examine the side effects of the use of corticosteroids. The results of the current clinical study show that the high-fat version of the DASH diet lowers blood pressure, but not LDL cholesterol.

BREAKFAST

1. Salmon and Egg Scramble

Preparation time: 15 minutes

Cooking time: 4 minutes

Servings: 4

Ingredients:

- 1 teaspoon of olive oil
- 3 organic whole eggs
- 3 tablespoons of water
- 1 minced garlic
- 6 Oz. Smoked salmon, sliced
- 2 avocados, sliced
- Black pepper to taste
- 1 green onion, chopped

Directions:

1. Warm-up olive oil in a large skillet and sauté onion in it. Take a medium bowl and whisk eggs in it, add water and make a scramble with the help of a fork. Add to the skillet the smoked salmon along with garlic and black pepper.

2. Stir for about 4 minutes until all ingredients get fluffy. At this stage, add the egg mixture. Once the eggs get firm, serve on a plate with a garnish of avocados.

Nutrition: Calories: 120, Carbs: 3g, Fat: 4g, Protein: 19g, Sodium: 898 mg, Potassium: 129mg

2. Pumpkin Muffins

Preparation time: 15 minutes

Cooking time: 20 minutes

Servings: 4

Ingredients:

- 4 cups of almond flour
- 2 cups of pumpkin, cooked and pureed
- 2 large whole organic eggs
- 3 teaspoons of baking powder
- 2 teaspoons of ground cinnamon
- 1/2 cup raw honey
- 4 teaspoons almond butter

Directions:

1. Preheat the oven at 400-degree F. Line the muffin paper on the muffin tray. Mix almond flour, pumpkin puree, eggs, baking powder, cinnamon, almond butter, and honey in a large bowl.

2. Put the prepared batter into a muffin tray and bake within 20 minutes. Once golden-brown, serve, and enjoy.

Nutrition: Calories: 136, Carbs: 22g, Fat: 5g, Protein: 2g, Sodium: 11 mg, Potassium: 699 mg

3. Sweet Berries Pancake

Preparation time: 15 minutes

Cooking time: 15 minutes

Servings: 4

Ingredients:

- 4 cups of almond flour
- Pinch of sea salt
- 2 organic eggs
- 4 teaspoons of walnut oil
- 1 cup of strawberries, mashed
- 1 cup of blueberries, mashed
- 1 teaspoon baking powder
- Honey for topping, optional

Directions:

1. Take a bowl and add almond flour, baking powder, and sea salt. Take another bowl and add eggs, walnut oil, strawberries, and blueberries mash. Combine ingredients of both bowls.

2. Heat a bit of walnut oil in a cooking pan and pour the spoonful mixture to make pancakes. Once the bubble comes on the top, flip the pancake to cook from the other side. Once done, serve with the glaze of honey on top.

Nutrition: Calories: 161, Carbs: 23g, Fat: 6g, Protein: 3g, Cholesterol: 82 mg, Sodium: 91 mg, Potassium: 252mg

4. Zucchini Pancakes

Preparation time: 15 minutes

Cooking time: 10 minutes

Servings: 4

Ingredients:

- 4 large zucchinis
- 4 green onions, diced
- 1/3 cup of milk
- 1 organic egg
- Sea Salt, just a pinch
- Black pepper, grated
- 2 tablespoons of olive oil

Directions:

1. First, wash the zucchinis and grate it with a cheese grater. Mix the egg and add in the grated zucchinis and milk in a large bowl. Warm oil in a skillet and sauté onions in it.

2. Put the egg batter into the skillet and make pancakes. Once cooked from both sides. Serve by sprinkling salt and pepper on top.

Nutrition: Calories: 70, Carbs: 8g, Fat: 3g, Protein: 2g, Cholesterol: 43 mg, Sodium: 60 mg, Potassium: 914mg

5. Breakfast Banana Split

Preparation time: 15 minutes

Cooking time: 0 minutes

Servings: 3

Ingredients:

- 2 bananas, peeled
- 1 cup oats, cooked
- 1/2 cup low-fat strawberry yogurt
- 1/3 teaspoon honey, optional
- 1/2 cup pineapple, chunks

Directions:

1. Peel the bananas and cut lengthwise. Place half of the banana in each separate bowl. Spoon strawberry yogurt on top and pour cooked oats with pineapple chunks on each banana. Serve immediately with a glaze of honey of liked.

Nutrition: Calories: 145, Carbs: 18g, Fat: 7g, Protein: 3g, Sodium: 2 mg, Potassium: 380 mg

6. Chilled Chicken, Artichoke and Zucchini Platter

Preparation time: 10 minutes

Cooking time: 5 minutes

Servings: 4

Ingredients:

- 2 medium chicken breasts, cooked and cut into 1-inch cubes
- ¼ cup extra virgin olive oil
- 2 cups artichoke hearts, drained and roughly chopped
- 3 large zucchini, diced/cut into small rounds
- 1 can (15 ounce) chickpeas
- 1 cup Kalamata olives

- ½ teaspoon Fresh ground black pepper
- ½ teaspoon Italian seasoning
- ¼ cup parmesan, grated

Directions:

1. Take a large skillet and place it over medium heat, heat up olive oil.

2. Add zucchini and sauté for 5 minutes, season with salt and pepper.

3. Remove from heat and add all the listed ingredients to the skillet.

4. Stir until combined.

5. Transfer to glass container and store.

6. Serve and enjoy!

Nutrition: Calories: 457; Fat: 22g; Carbohydrates: 30g; Protein: 24g

7. Chicken and Carrot Stew

Preparation time: 15 minutes

Cooking time: 6 hours

Servings: 6

Ingredients:

- 4 chicken breasts, boneless and cubed
- 2 cups chicken broth
- 1 cup tomatoes, chopped
- 3 cups carrots, peeled and cubed
- 1 teaspoon thyme dried
- 1 cup onion, chopped
- 2 garlic clove, minced
- Pepper to taste

Directions:

1. Add all the ingredients to the Slow Cooker.
2. Stir and close the lid.
3. Cook for 6 hours.
4. Serve hot and enjoy!

Nutrition: Calories: 182; Fat: 4g; Carbohydrates: 10g; Protein: 39g

8. Tasty Spinach Pie

Preparation time: 10 minutes

Cooking time: 4 hours

Servings: 2

Ingredients:

- 10 ounces spinach
- 2 cups baby Bella mushrooms, chopped
- 1 red bell pepper, chopped
- 1 ½ cups low-fat cheese, shredded
- 8 whole eggs
- 1 cup coconut cream
- 2 tablespoons chives, chopped
- Pinch of pepper
- ½ cup almond flour
- ¼ teaspoon baking soda

Directions:

1. Take a bowl and add eggs, coconut cream, chives, pepper and whisk well.
2. Add almond flour, baking soda, cheese, mushrooms bell pepper, spinach and toss well.
3. Grease your cooker and transfer mix to the Slow Cooker.
4. Place lid and cook on LOW for 4 hours.

5. Slice and enjoy!

Nutrition: Calories: 201; Fat: 6g; Carbohydrates: 8g; Protein: 5g

9. Mesmerizing Carrot and Pineapple Mix

Preparation time: 10 minutes

Cooking time: 6 hours

Servings: 10

Ingredients:

- 1 cup raisins
- 6 cups water
- 23 ounces natural applesauce
- 2 tablespoons stevia
- 2 tablespoons cinnamon powder
- 14 ounces carrots, shredded
- 8 ounces canned pineapple, crushed
- 1 tablespoon pumpkin pie spice

Directions:

1. Add carrots, applesauce, raisins, stevia, cinnamon, pineapple, pumpkin pie spice to your Slow Cooker and gently stir.
2. Place lid and cook on LOW for 6 hours.
3. Serve and enjoy!

Nutrition: Calories: 179; Fat: 5g; Carbohydrates: 15g; Protein: 4g

10. Blackberry Chicken Wings

Preparation time: 35 minutes

Cooking time: 50 minutes

Servings: 4

Ingredients:

- 3 pounds chicken wings, about 20 pieces
- ½ cup blackberry chipotle jam
- Sunflower seeds and pepper to taste
- ½ cup water

Directions:

1. Add water and jam to a bowl and mix well.
2. Place chicken wings in a zip bag and add two-thirds of the marinade.
3. Season with sunflower seeds and pepper.
4. Let it marinate for 30 minutes.
5. Pre-heat your oven to 400 degrees F.
6. Prepare a baking sheet and wire rack, place chicken wings in wire rack and bake for 15 minutes.
7. Brush remaining marinade and bake for 30 minutes more.
8. Enjoy!

Nutrition: Calories: 502; Fat: 39g; Carbohydrates: 01.8g; Protein: 34g

11. Chipotle Lettuce Chicken

Preparation time: 10 minutes

Cooking time: 25 minutes

Servings: 6

Ingredients:

- 1 pound chicken breast, cut into strips
- Splash of olive oil
- 1 red onion, finely sliced
- 14 ounces tomatoes
- 1 teaspoon chipotle, chopped
- ½ teaspoon cumin
- Lettuce as needed
- Fresh coriander leaves

- Jalapeno chilies, sliced
- Fresh tomato slices for garnish
- Lime wedges

Directions:

1. Take a non-stick frying pan and place it over medium heat.
2. Add oil and heat it up.
3. Add chicken and cook until brown.
4. Keep the chicken on the side.
5. Add tomatoes, sugar, chipotle, cumin to the same pan and simmer for 25 minutes until you have a nice sauce.
6. Add chicken into the sauce and cook for 5 minutes.
7. Transfer the mix to another place.
8. Use lettuce wraps to take a portion of the mixture and serve with a squeeze of lemon.
9. Enjoy!

Nutrition: Calories: 332; Fat: 15g; Carbohydrates: 13g; Protein: 34g

12. Balsamic Chicken and Vegetables

Preparation time: 15 minutes

Cooking time: 25 minutes

Servings: 2

Ingredients:

- 4 chicken thigh, boneless and skinless
- 5 stalks of asparagus, halved
- 1 pepper, cut in chunks
- 1/2 red onion, diced
- ½ cup carrots, sliced
- 1 garlic cloves, minced
- 2-ounces mushrooms, diced
- ¼ cup balsamic vinegar
- 1 tablespoon olive oil
- ½ teaspoon stevia
- ½ tablespoon oregano
- Sunflower seeds and pepper as needed

Directions:

1. Pre-heat your oven to 425 degrees F.
2. Take a bowl and add all of the vegetables and mix.
3. Add spices and oil and mix.
4. Dip the chicken pieces into spice mix and coat them well.

5. Place the veggies and chicken onto a pan in a single layer.

6. Cook for 25 minutes.

7. Serve and enjoy!

Nutrition: Calories: 401; Fat: 17g; Net Carbohydrates: 11g; Protein: 48g

13. Cream Dredged Corn Platter

Preparation time: 10 minutes

Cooking time: 4 hours

Servings: 3

Ingredients:

- 3 cups corn
- 2 ounces cream cheese, cubed
- 2 tablespoons milk
- 2 tablespoons whipping cream
- 2 tablespoons butter, melted
- Salt and pepper as needed
- 1 tablespoon green onion, chopped

Directions:

1. Add corn, cream cheese, milk, whipping cream, butter, salt and pepper to your Slow Cooker.
2. Give it a nice toss to mix everything well.
3. Place lid and cook on LOW for 4 hours.
4. Divide the mix amongst serving platters.
5. Serve and enjoy!

Nutrition: Calories: 261; Fat: 11g; Carbohydrates: 17g; Protein: 6g

14. Exuberant Sweet Potatoes

Preparation time: 5 minutes

Cooking time: 7-8 hours

Servings: 4

Ingredients:

- 6 sweet potatoes, washed and dried

Directions:

1. Loosely ball up 7-8 pieces of aluminum foil in the bottom of your Slow Cooker, covering about half of the surface area.
2. Prick each potato 6-8 times using a fork.
3. Wrap each potato with foil and seal them.
4. Place wrapped potatoes in the cooker on top of the foil bed.
5. Place lid and cook on LOW for 7-8 hours.
6. Use tongs to remove the potatoes and unwrap them.
7. Serve and enjoy!

Nutrition: Calories: 129; Fat: 0g; Carbohydrates: 30g; Protein: 2g

15. Ethiopian Cabbage Delight

Preparation time: 15 minutes

Cooking time: 6-8 hours

Servings: 6

Ingredients:

- ½ cup water
- 1 head green cabbage, cored and chopped
- 1 pound sweet potatoes, peeled and chopped
- 3 carrots, peeled and chopped
- 1 onion, sliced
- 1 teaspoon extra virgin olive oil
- ½ teaspoon ground turmeric
- ½ teaspoon ground cumin
- ¼ teaspoon ground ginger

Directions:

1. Add water to your Slow Cooker.
2. Take a medium bowl and add cabbage, carrots, sweet potatoes, onion and mix.
3. Add olive oil, turmeric, ginger, cumin and toss until the veggies are fully coated.
4. Transfer veggie mix to your Slow Cooker.
5. Cover and cook on LOW for 6-8 hours.
6. Serve and enjoy!

Nutrition: Calories: 155; Fat: 2g; Carbohydrates: 35g; Protein: 4g

MAINS

16. Eggplant Parmesan Stacks

Preparation time: 15 minutes

Cooking time: 20 minutes

Servings: 4

Ingredients:

- 1 large eggplant, cut into thick slices
- 2 tablespoons olive oil, divided
- ¼ teaspoon kosher or sea salt
- ¼ teaspoon ground black pepper
- 1 cup panko bread crumbs
- ¼ cup freshly grated Parmesan cheese
- 5 to 6 garlic cloves, minced
- ½ pound fresh mozzarella, sliced
- 1½ cups lower-sodium marinara
- ½ cup fresh basil leaves, torn

Directions:

1. Preheat the oven to 425°F. Coat the eggplant slices in 1 tablespoon olive oil and sprinkle with the salt and black pepper. Put on a large baking sheet, then roast for 10 to 12 minutes, until soft with crispy edges. Remove the eggplant and set the oven to a low broil.

2. In a bowl, stir the remaining tablespoon of olive oil, bread crumbs, Parmesan cheese, and garlic. Remove the cooled eggplant from the baking sheet and clean it.

3. Create layers on the same baking sheet by stacking a roasted eggplant slice with a slice of mozzarella, a tablespoon of marinara, and a tablespoon of the bread crumb mixture, repeating with 2 layers of each ingredient. Cook under the broiler within 3 to 4 minutes until the cheese is melted and bubbly.

Nutrition: Calories: 377, Fat: 22g, Sodium: 509mg, Carbohydrate: 29g, Protein: 16g

17. Roasted Vegetable Enchiladas

Preparation time: 15 minutes

Cooking time: 45 minutes

Servings: 8

Ingredients:

- 2 zucchinis, diced
- 1 red bell pepper, seeded and sliced
- 1 red onion, peeled and sliced
- 2 ears corn
- 2 tablespoons canola oil
- 1 can no-salt-added black beans, drained
- 1½ tablespoons chili powder
- 2 teaspoon ground cumin
- 1/8 teaspoon kosher or sea salt
- ½ teaspoon ground black pepper
- 8 (8-inch) whole-wheat tortillas
- 1 cup Enchilada Sauce or store-bought enchilada sauce
- ½ cup shredded Mexican-style cheese
- ½ cup plain nonfat Greek yogurt
- ½ cup cilantro leaves, chopped

Directions:

1. Preheat oven to 400°F. Place the zucchini, red bell pepper, and red onion on a baking sheet. Place the ears

of corn separately on the same baking sheet. Drizzle all with the canola oil and toss to coat. Roast for 10 to 12 minutes, until the vegetables are tender. Remove and reduce the temperature to 375°F.

2. Cut the corn from the cob. Transfer the corn kernels, zucchini, red bell pepper, and onion to a bowl and stir in the black beans, chili powder, cumin, salt, and black pepper until combined.

3. Oiled a 9-by-13-inch baking dish with cooking spray. Line up the tortillas in the greased baking dish. Evenly distribute the vegetable bean filling into each tortilla. Pour half of the enchilada sauce and sprinkle half of the shredded cheese on top of the filling.

4. Roll each tortilla into enchilada shape and place them seam-side down. Pour the remaining enchilada sauce and sprinkle the remaining cheese over the enchiladas. Bake for 25 minutes until the cheese is melted and bubbly. Serve the enchiladas with Greek yogurt and chopped cilantro.

Nutrition: Calories: 335, Fat: 15g, Sodium: 557mg, Carbohydrate: 42g, Protein: 13g

18. Lentil Avocado Tacos

Preparation time: 15 minutes

Cooking time: 35 minutes

Servings: 6

Ingredients:

- 1 tablespoon canola oil
- ½ yellow onion, peeled and diced
- 2-3 garlic cloves, minced
- 1½ cups dried lentils
- ½ teaspoon kosher or sea salt
- 3 to 3½ cups unsalted vegetable or chicken stock
- 2½ tablespoons Taco Seasoning or store-bought low-sodium taco seasoning
- 16 (6-inch) corn tortillas, toasted
- 2 ripe avocados, peeled and sliced

Directions:

1. Heat-up the canola oil in a large skillet or Dutch oven over medium heat. Cook the onion within 4 to 5 minutes, until soft. Mix in the garlic and cook within 30 seconds until fragrant. Then add the lentils, salt, and stock. Bring to a simmer for 25 to 35 minutes, adding additional stock if needed.

2. When there's only a small amount of liquid left in the pan, and the lentils are al dente, stir in the taco

seasoning and let simmer for 1 to 2 minutes. Taste and adjust the seasoning, if necessary. Spoon the lentil mixture into tortillas and serve with the avocado slices.

Nutrition: Calories: 400, Fat: 14g, Sodium: 336mg, Carbohydrate: 64g, Fiber: 15g, Protein: 16g

19. Tomato & Olive Orecchiette with Basil Pesto

Preparation time: 15 minutes

Cooking time: 25 minutes

Servings: 6

Ingredients:

- 12 ounces orecchiette pasta
- 2 tablespoons olive oil
- 1-pint cherry tomatoes, quartered
- ½ cup Basil Pesto or store-bought pesto
- ¼ cup Kalamata olives, sliced
- 1 tablespoon dried oregano leaves
- ¼ teaspoon kosher or sea salt
- ½ teaspoon freshly cracked black pepper
- ¼ teaspoon crushed red pepper flakes
- 2 tablespoons freshly grated Parmesan cheese

Directions:

1. Boil a large pot of water. Cook the orecchiette, drain and transfer the pasta to a large nonstick skillet.

2. Put the skillet over medium-low heat, then heat the olive oil. Stir in the cherry tomatoes, pesto, olives, oregano, salt, black pepper, and crushed red pepper flakes. Cook within 8 to 10 minutes, until heated

throughout. Serve the pasta with the freshly grated Parmesan cheese.

Nutrition: Calories: 332, Fat: 13g, Sodium: 389mg, Carbohydrate: 44g, Protein: 9g

20. Italian Stuffed Portobello Mushroom Burgers

Preparation time: 15 minutes

Cooking time: 25 minutes

Servings: 4

Ingredients:

- 1 tablespoon olive oil
- 4 large portobello mushrooms, washed and dried
- ½ yellow onion, peeled and diced
- 4 garlic cloves, peeled and minced
- 1 can cannellini beans, drained
- ½ cup fresh basil leaves, torn
- ½ cup panko bread crumbs
- 1/8 teaspoon kosher or sea salt
- ¼ teaspoon ground black pepper
- 1 cup lower-sodium marinara, divided
- ½ cup shredded mozzarella cheese
- 4 whole-wheat buns, toasted
- 1 cup fresh arugula

Directions:

1. Heat-up the olive oil in a large skillet to medium-high heat. Sear the mushrooms for 4 to 5 minutes per side,

until slightly soft. Place on a baking sheet. Preheat the oven to a low broil.

2. Put the onion in the skillet and cook for 4 to 5 minutes, until slightly soft. Mix in the garlic then cooks within 30 to 60 seconds. Move the onions plus garlic to a bowl. Add the cannellini beans and smash with the back of a fork to form a chunky paste. Stir in the basil, bread crumbs, salt, and black pepper and half of the marinara. Cook for 5 minutes.

3. Remove the bean mixture from the stove and divide among the mushroom caps. Spoon the remaining marinara over the stuffed mushrooms and top each with the mozzarella cheese. Broil within 3 to 4 minutes, until the cheese is melted and bubbly. Transfer the burgers to the toasted whole-wheat buns and top with the arugula.

Nutrition: Calories: 407, Fat: 9g, Sodium: 575mg, Carbohydrate: 63g, Protein: 25g

SIDES & APPETIZERS

21. Spicy Brussels sprouts

Preparation time: 10 minutes

Cooking time: 20 minutes

Servings: 6

Ingredients:

- 2 pounds Brussels sprouts, halved
- 2 tablespoons olive oil
- A pinch of black pepper
- 1 tablespoon sesame oil
- 2 garlic cloves, minced
- ½ cup coconut aminos
- 2 teaspoons apple cider vinegar
- 1 tablespoon coconut sugar
- 2 teaspoons chili sauce
- A pinch of red pepper flakes
- Sesame seeds for serving

Directions:

1. Spread the sprouts on a lined baking dish, add the olive oil, the sesame oil, black pepper, garlic, aminos, vinegar, coconut sugar, chili sauce, and pepper flakes, toss well, introduce in the oven and bake within 20

minutes at 425 degrees F. Divide the sprouts between plates, sprinkle sesame seeds on top and serve as a side dish.

Nutrition: Calories: 64; Carbs: 13g; Fat: 0g; Protein: 4g; Sodium: 314 mg

22. Baked Cauliflower with Chili

Preparation time: 10 minutes

Cooking time: 30 minutes

Servings: 4

Ingredients:

- 3 tablespoons olive oil
- 2 tablespoons chili sauce
- Juice of 1 lime
- 3 garlic cloves, minced
- 1 cauliflower head, florets separated
- A pinch of black pepper
- 1 teaspoon cilantro, chopped

Directions:

1. In a bowl, combine the oil with the chili sauce, lime juice, garlic, and black pepper and whisk. Add cauliflower florets, toss, spread on a lined baking sheet, introduce in the oven and bake at 425 degrees F for 30 minutes. Divide the cauliflower between plates, sprinkle cilantro on top, and serve as a side dish.

Nutrition: Calories: 31; Carbs: 3g; Fat: 0g; Protein: 3g; Sodium: 4 mg

23. __Baked Broccoli__

Preparation time: 10 minutes

Cooking time: 15 minutes

Servings: 4

Ingredients:

- 1 tablespoon olive oil
- 1 broccoli head, florets separated
- 2 garlic cloves, minced
- ½ cup coconut cream
- ½ cup low-fat mozzarella, shredded
- ¼ cup low-fat parmesan, grated
- A pinch of pepper flakes, crushed

Directions:

1. In a baking dish, combine the broccoli with oil, garlic, cream, pepper flakes, mozzarella, and toss. Sprinkle the parmesan on top, introduce in the oven and bake at 375 degrees F for 15 minutes. Serve.

Nutrition: Calories: 90; Carbs: 6g; Fat: 7g; Protein: 3g; Sodium: 30 mg

24. Slow Cooked Potatoes with Cheddar

Preparation time: 10 minutes

Cooking time: 6 hours

Servings: 6

Ingredients:

- Cooking spray
- 2 pounds baby potatoes, quartered
- 3 cups low-fat cheddar cheese, shredded
- 2 garlic cloves, minced
- 8 bacon slices, cooked and chopped
- ¼ cup green onions, chopped
- 1 tablespoon sweet paprika
- A pinch of black pepper

Directions:

1. Spray a slow cooker with the cooking spray, add baby potatoes, cheddar, garlic, bacon, green onions, paprika, and black pepper, toss, cover, and cook on High for 6 hours. Serve.

Nutrition: Calories: 112; Carbs: 26g; Fat: 4g; Protein: 8g; Sodium: 234 mg

25. Squash Salad with Orange

Preparation time: 10 minutes

Cooking time: 30 minutes

Servings: 6

Ingredients:

- 1 cup of orange juice
- 3 tablespoons coconut sugar
- 1 and ½ tablespoons mustard
- 1 tablespoon ginger, grated
- 1 and ½ pounds butternut squash, peeled and roughly cubed
- Cooking spray
- A pinch of black pepper
- 1/3 cup olive oil
- 6 cups salad greens
- 1 radicchio, sliced
- ½ cup pistachios, roasted

Directions:

1. Mix the orange juice with the sugar, mustard, ginger, black pepper, squash in a bowl, toss well, spread on a lined baking sheet, spray everything with cooking oil, and bake for 30 minutes 400 degrees F.

2. In a salad bowl, combine the squash with salad greens, radicchio, pistachios, and oil, toss well, and then serve.

Nutrition: Calories: 17; Carbs: 2g; Fat: 0g; Protein: 0g; Sodium: 0 mg

SEAFOOD

26. Salmon with Peas and Parsley Dressing

Preparation time: 15 minutes

Cooking Time: 15 minutes

Serving: 4

Ingredients:

- 16 ounces salmon fillets, boneless and skin-on
- tablespoon parsley, chopped
- 10 ounces peas
- 9 ounces vegetable stock, low sodium
- cups water
- ½ teaspoon oregano, dried
- ½ teaspoon sweet paprika
- garlic cloves, minced
- A pinch of black pepper

Directions:

1. Add garlic, parsley, paprika, oregano and stock to a food processor and blend.
2. Add water to your Instant Pot.
3. Add steam basket.
4. Add fish fillets inside the steamer basket.

5. Season with pepper.

6. Lock the lid and cook on HIGH pressure for 10 minutes.

7. Release the pressure naturally over 10 minutes.

8. Divide the fish amongst plates.

9. Add peas to the steamer basket and lock the lid again, cook on HIGH pressure for 5 minutes.

10. Quick release the pressure.

11. Divide the peas next to your fillets and serve with the parsley dressing drizzled on top

12. Enjoy!

Nutrition: Calories: 315; Fat: 5g; Carbohydrates: 14g; Protein: 16g

27. Mackerel and Orange Medley

Preparation time: 10 minutes

Cooking Time: 10 minutes

Serving: 4

Ingredients:

- 4 mackerel fillets, skinless and boneless
- 4 spring onion, chopped
- teaspoon olive oil
- 1-inch ginger piece, grated
- Black pepper as needed
- Juice and zest of 1 whole orange
- 1 cup low sodium fish stock

Directions:

1. Season the fillets with black pepper and rub olive oil.
2. Add stock, orange juice, ginger, orange zest and onion to Instant Pot.
3. Place a steamer basket and add the fillets.
4. Lock the lid and cook on HIGH pressure for 10 minutes.
5. Release the pressure naturally over 10 minutes.
6. Divide the fillets amongst plates and drizzle the orange sauce from the pot over the fish.
7. Enjoy!

Nutrition: Calories: 200; Fat: 4g; Carbohydrates: 19g; Protein: 14g

28. Spicy Chili Salmon

Preparation time: 10 minutes

Cooking Time: 7 minutes

Serving: 4

Ingredients:

- 4 salmon fillets, boneless and skin-on
- 2 tablespoons assorted chili peppers, chopped
- Juice of 1 lemon
- lemon, sliced
- 1 cup water
- Black pepper

Directions:

1. Add water to the Instant Pot.
2. Add steamer basket and add salmon fillets, season the fillets with salt and pepper.
3. Drizzle lemon juice on top.
4. Top with lemon slices.
5. Lock the lid and cook on HIGH pressure for 7 minutes.
6. Release the pressure naturally over 10 minutes.
7. Divide the salmon and lemon slices between serving plates.
8. Enjoy!

Nutrition: Calories: 281; Fats: 8g; Carbs: 19g; Protein: 7g

29. Simple One Pot Mussels

Preparation time: 10 minutes

Cooking Time: 5 minutes

Serving: 4

Ingredients:

- 2 tablespoons butter
- 2 chopped shallots
- 4 minced garlic cloves
- ½ cup broth
- ½ cup white wine
- 2 pounds cleaned mussels
- Lemon and parsley for serving

Directions:

1. Clean the mussels and remove the beard.
2. Discard any mussels that do not close when tapped against a hard surface.
3. Set your pot to Sauté mode and add chopped onion and butter.
4. Stir and sauté onions.
5. Add garlic and cook for 1 minute.
6. Add broth and wine.
7. Lock the lid and cook for 5 minutes on HIGH pressure.
8. Release the pressure naturally over 10 minutes.

9. Serve with a sprinkle of parsley and enjoy!

Nutrition: Calories: 286; Fats: 14g; Carbs: 12g; Protein: 28g

30. Lemon Pepper and Salmon

Preparation time: 5 minutes

Cooking Time: 6 minutes

Serving: 3

Ingredients:

- ¾ cup water
- Few sprigs of parsley, basil, tarragon, basil
- pound of salmon, skin on
- teaspoons ghee
- ¼ teaspoon salt
- ½ teaspoon pepper
- ½ lemon, thinly sliced
- 1 whole carrot, julienned

Directions:

1. Set your pot to Sauté mode and water and herbs.
2. Place a steamer rack inside your pot and place salmon.
3. Drizzle the ghee on top of the salmon and season with salt and pepper.
4. Cover lemon slices.
5. Lock the lid and cook on HIGH pressure for 3 minutes.
6. Release the pressure naturally over 10 minutes.
7. Transfer the salmon to a serving platter.
8. Set your pot to Sauté mode and add vegetables.

9. Cook for 1-2 minutes.

10. Serve with vegetables and salmon.

11. Enjoy!

Nutrition: Calories: 464; Fat: 34g; Carbohydrates: 3g; Protein: 34g

POULTRY

31. Salsa Chicken Chili

Preparation time: 15 minutes

Cooking time: 20 minutes

Servings: 8

Ingredients:

- 2 1/2 lbs. chicken breasts, skinless and boneless
- 1/2 tsp. cumin powder
- 3 garlic cloves, minced
- 1 onion, diced
- 16 oz. salsa
- 1 tsp. oregano
- 1 tbsp. olive oil

Directions:

1. Add oil into the instant pot and set the pot on sauté mode. Add onion to the pot and sauté until softened, about 3 minutes. Add garlic and sauté for a minute. Add oregano and cumin and sauté for a minute. Add half salsa and stir well. Place chicken and pour remaining salsa over chicken.

2. Seal pot with the lid and select manual and set timer for 10 minutes. Remove chicken and shred. Move it back to the pot, then stir well to combine. Serve and enjoy.

Nutrition: Calories: 308 Fat: 12.4g Protein: 42.1g Carbs: 5.4g
Sodium 656 mg

32. Honey Crusted Chicken

Preparation time: 10 minutes

Cooking time: 25 minutes

Servings: 2

Ingredients:

- 1 teaspoon paprika
- 8 saltine crackers, 2 inches square
- 2 chicken breasts, each 4 ounces
- 4 tsp. honey

Directions:

1. Set the oven to heat at 375 degrees F. Grease a baking dish with cooking oil. Smash the crackers in a Zip lock bag and toss them with paprika in a bowl. Brush chicken with honey and add it to the crackers.

2. Mix well and transfer the chicken to the baking dish. Bake the chicken for 25 minutes until golden brown. Serve.

Nutrition: Calories 219 Fat 17 g Sodium 456 mg Carbs 12.1 g Protein 31 g

33. Paella with Chicken, Leeks, and Tarragon

Preparation time: 10 minutes

Cooking time: 20 minutes

Servings: 2

Ingredients:

- 1 teaspoon extra-virgin olive oil
- 1 small onion, sliced
- 2 leeks (whites only), thinly sliced
- 3 garlic cloves, minced
- 1-pound boneless, skinless chicken breast, cut into strips 1/2-inch-wide and 2 inches long
- 2 large tomatoes, chopped
- 1 red pepper, sliced
- 2/3 cup long-grain brown rice
- 1 teaspoon tarragon, or to taste
- 2 cups fat-free, unsalted chicken broth
- 1 cup frozen peas
- 1/4 cup chopped fresh parsley
- 1 lemon, cut into 4 wedges

Directions:

1. Preheat a nonstick pan with olive oil over medium heat. Toss in leeks, onions, chicken strips, and garlic.

Sauté for 5 minutes. Stir in red pepper slices and tomatoes. Stir and cook for 5 minutes.

2. Add tarragon, broth, and rice. Let it boil, then reduce the heat to a simmer. Continue cooking for 10 minutes, then add peas and continue cooking until the liquid is thoroughly cooked. Garnish with parsley and lemon. Serve.

Nutrition: Calories 388 Fat 15.2 g Sodium 572 mg Carbs 5.4 g Protein 27 g

MEAT

34. Citrus Pork

Preparation time: 10 minutes

Cooking time: 30 minutes

Servings: 4

Ingredients:

- Zest of 2 limes, grated
- Zest of 1 orange, grated
- Juice of 1 orange
- Juice of 2 limes
- 4 teaspoons garlic, minced
- ¾ cup olive oil
- 1 cup cilantro, chopped
- 1 cup mint, chopped
- Black pepper to the taste
- 4 pork loin steaks

Directions:

1. In your food processor, mix lime zest and juice with orange zest and juice, garlic, oil, cilantro, mint and pepper and blend well.

2. Put the steaks in a bowl, add the citrus mix and toss really well.

3. Heat up a pan over medium-high heat, add pork steaks and the marinade, cook for 4 minutes on each side, introduce the pan in the oven and bake at 350 degrees F for 20 minutes.

4. Divide the steaks between plates, drizzle some of the cooking juices all over and serve with a side salad.

5. Enjoy!

Nutrition: Calories 270, Fat 7, Fiber 2, Carbs 8, Protein 20

35. **Pork Chops with Nutmeg**

Preparation time: 10 minutes

Cooking time: 40 minutes

Servings: 3

Ingredients:

- 8 ounces mushrooms, sliced
- ¼ cup coconut milk
- 1 teaspoon garlic powder
- 1 yellow onion, chopped
- 3 pork chops, boneless
- 2 teaspoons nutmeg, ground
- 1 tablespoon balsamic vinegar
- ½ cup olive oil

Directions:

1. Heat up a pan with the oil over medium heat, add mushrooms and onions, stir and cook for 5 minutes.
2. Add pork chops, nutmeg and garlic powder and cook for 5 minutes more.
3. Add vinegar and coconut milk, toss, introduce in the oven and bake at 350 degrees F and bake for 30 minutes.
4. Divide between plates and serve.
5. Enjoy!

Nutrition: Calories 260, Fat 10, Fiber 6, Carbs 8, Protein 22

36. Italian Parmesan Pork

Preparation time: 10 minutes

Cooking time: 30 minutes

Servings: 6

Ingredients:

- 2 tablespoons parsley, chopped
- 1 pound pork cutlets, thinly sliced
- 1 tablespoon olive oil
- ¼ cup yellow onion, chopped
- 3 garlic cloves, minced
- 2 tablespoons parmesan, grated
- 15 ounces canned tomatoes, no-salt-added and chopped
- 1/3 cup low sodium chicken stock
- Black pepper to the taste
- 1 teaspoon Italian seasoning

Directions:

1. Heat up a pan with the oil over medium-high heat, add pork cutlets, season with Italian seasoning and black pepper and cook for 4 minutes on each side.

2. Add onion, garlic, tomatoes, stock and top with parmesan, introduce the pan in the oven and bake at 350 degrees F for 20 minutes.

3. Sprinkle parsley on top, divide everything between plates and serve.

4. Enjoy!

Nutrition: Calories 280, Fat 17, Fiber 5, Carbs 12, Protein 34

37. Pork Roast with Cranberry

Preparation time: 10 minutes

Cooking time: 1 hour and 30 minutes

Servings: 4

Ingredients:

- 1 tablespoon coconut flour
- Black pepper to the taste
- 1 and ½ pounds pork loin roast
- ½ teaspoon ginger, grated
- ½ cup cranberries
- 2 garlic cloves, minced
- Juice of ½ lemon
- ½ cup low-sodium veggie stock

Directions:

1. Put the stock in a small pan, heat it up over medium-high heat, add black pepper, ginger, garlic, cranberries, lemon juice and the flour, whisk well and cook for 10 minutes.

2. Put the roast in a pan, add the cranberry sauce on top, introduce in the oven and bake at 375 degrees F for 1 hour and 20 minutes.

3. Slice the roast, divide it and the sauce between plates and serve.

4. Enjoy!

Nutrition: Calories 330, Fat 13, Fiber 2, Carbs 13, Protein 25

38. Pork Patties

Preparation time: 10 minutes

Cooking time: 35 minutes

Servings: 6

Ingredients:

- ½ cup coconut flour
- 2 tablespoons olive oil
- 2 egg, whisked
- Black pepper to the taste
- 1 and ½ pounds pork, ground
- 10 ounces low sodium veggie stock
- ¼ cup tomato sauce, no-salt-added
- ½ teaspoon mustard powder

Directions:

1. Put the flour in a bowl and the egg in another one.
2. Mix the pork with black pepper and a pinch of paprika, shape medium patties out of this mix, dip them in the egg and then dredge in flour.
3. Heat up a pan with the oil over medium-high heat, add the patties and cook them for 5 minutes on each side.
4. In a bowl, combine the stock with tomato sauce and mustard powder and whisk.

5. Add this over the patties, cook for 10 minutes over medium heat, divide everything between plates and serve.

6. Enjoy!

Nutrition: Calories 332, Fat 18, Fiber 4, Carbs 11, Protein 25

VEGETABLES

39. Chunky Black-Bean Dip

Preparation time: 5 minutes

Cooking time: 1 minute

Servings: 2

Ingredients:

- 1 (15-ounce) can black beans, drained, with liquid reserved
- ½-can of chipotle peppers in adobo sauce
- ¼ cup plain Greek yogurt
- Freshly ground black pepper

Directions:

1. Combine beans, peppers, and yogurt in a food processor or blender and process until smooth. Add some of the bean liquid, 1 tablespoon at a time, for a thinner consistency. Season to taste with black pepper. Serve.

Nutrition: Calories: 70g; Fat: 1g; Sodium: 159mg; Carbohydrate: 11g; Protein: 5g

40. Classic Hummus

Preparation time: 5 minutes

Cooking time: 0 minutes

Servings: 6–8

Ingredients:

- 1 (15-ounce) can chickpeas, drained and rinsed
- 3 tablespoons sesame tahini
- 2 tablespoons olive oil
- 3 garlic cloves, chopped
- Juice of 1 lemon
- Salt
- Freshly ground black pepper

Directions:

1. Mix all the ingredients until smooth but thick in a food processor or blender. Add water if necessary to produce a smoother hummus. Store covered for up to 5 days.

Nutrition: Calories: 147g; Fat: 10g; Sodium: 64mg; Carbohydrate: 11g; Protein: 6g.

41. Crispy Potato Skins

Preparation time: 2 minutes

Cooking time: 19 minutes

Servings: 2

Ingredients:

- 2 russet potatoes
- Cooking spray
- 1 teaspoon dried rosemary
- 1/8 teaspoon freshly ground black pepper

Directions:

1. Preheat the oven to 375°f. Prick or pierce the potatoes all over using a fork. Put on a plate. Cook on full power in the microwave within 5 minutes. Flip over, and cook again within 3 to 4 minutes more, or until soft.

2. Carefully—the potatoes will be very hot—scoop out the pulp of the potatoes, leaving a 1/8 inch of potato pulp attached to the skin. Set aside.

3. Spray the inside of each potato with cooking spray. Press in the rosemary and pepper. Place the skins on a baking sheet and bake in a preheated oven for 5 to 10 minutes until slightly browned and crispy. Serve immediately.

Nutrition: Calories 114; Fat: 0g; Sodium: 0mg; Carbohydrate: 27g; Protein: 3g

42. Roasted Chickpeas

Preparation time: 5 minutes

Cooking time: 30 minutes

Servings: 2

Ingredients:

- 1 (15-ounce can) chickpeas, drained and rinsed
- ½ teaspoon olive oil
- 2 teaspoons of your favorite herbs or spice blend
- ¼ teaspoon salt

Directions:

1. Preheat the oven to 400°f.

2. Wrap a rimmed baking sheet with paper towels, place the chickpeas on it in an even layer, and blot with more paper towels until most of the liquid is absorbed.

3. In a medium bowl, gently toss the chickpeas and olive oil until combined. Sprinkle the mixture with the herbs and salt and toss again.

4. Place the chickpeas back on the baking sheet and spread in an even layer. Bake for 30 to 40 minutes, until crunchy and golden brown. Stir halfway through. Serve.

Nutrition: Calories: 175g; Fat: 3g; Sodium: 474mg; Carbohydrate: 29g; Protein: 11g

43. Carrot-Cake Smoothie

Preparation time 5 minutes

Cooking time: 0 minutes

Servings: 2

Ingredients:

- 1 frozen banana, peeled and diced
- 1 cup carrots, diced (peeled if preferred)
- 1 cup nonfat or low-fat milk
- ½ cup nonfat or low-fat vanilla Greek yogurt
- ½ cup ice
- ¼ cup diced pineapple, frozen
- ½ teaspoon ground cinnamon
- Pinch nutmeg
- Optional toppings: chopped walnuts, grated carrots

Directions:

1. Process all of the fixings to a blender. Serve immediately with optional toppings as desired.

Nutrition: Calories: 180g; Fat: 1g; Sodium: 114mg; Carbohydrate: 36g; Protein 10g

SNACK AND DESSERT

44. Coconut Figs

Preparation time: 6 minutes

Cooking time: 5 minutes

Servings: 4

Ingredients:

- 2 tablespoons coconut butter
- 12 figs, halved
- ¼ cup coconut sugar
- 1 cup almonds, toasted and chopped

Directions:

1. Put butter in a pot, heat up over medium heat, add sugar, whisk well, also add almonds and figs, toss, cook for 5 minutes, divide into small cups and serve cold.
2. Enjoy!

Nutrition: Calories 150, Fat 4, Fiber 5, Carbs 7, Protein 4

45. Lemony Banana Mix

Preparation time: 10 minutes

Cooking time: 0 minutes

Servings: 4

Ingredients:

- 4 bananas, peeled and chopped
- 5 strawberries, halved
- Juice of 2 lemons
- 4 tablespoons coconut sugar

Directions:

1. In a bowl, combine the bananas with the strawberries, lemon juice and sugar, toss and serve cold.
2. Enjoy!

Nutrition: Calories 172, Fat 7, Fiber 5, Carbs 5, Protein 5

46. Cocoa Banana Dessert Smoothie

Preparation time: 5 minutes

Cooking time: 0 minutes

Servings: 2

Ingredients:

- 2 medium bananas, peeled
- 2 teaspoons cocoa powder
- ½ big avocado, pitted, peeled and mashed
- ¾ cup almond milk

Directions:

1. In your blender, combine the bananas with the cocoa, avocado and milk, pulse well, divide into 2 glasses and serve.
2. Enjoy!

Nutrition: Calories 155, Fat 3, Fiber 4, Carbs 6, Protein 5

47. Kiwi Bars

Preparation time: 30 minutes

Cooking time: 0 minutes

Servings: 4

Ingredients:

- 1 cup olive oil
- 1 and ½ bananas, peeled and chopped
- 1/3 cup coconut sugar
- ¼ cup lemon juice
- 1 teaspoon lemon zest, grated
- 3 kiwis, peeled and chopped

Directions:

1. In your food processor, mix bananas with kiwis, almost all the oil, sugar, lemon juice and lemon zest and pulse well.
2. Grease a pan with the remaining oil, pour the kiwi mix, spread, keep in the fridge for 30 minutes, slice and serve,
3. Enjoy!

Nutrition: Calories 207, Fat 3, Fiber 3, Carbs 4, Protein 4

48. Black Tea Bars

Preparation time: 10 minutes

Cooking time: 35 minutes

Servings: 12

Ingredients:

- 6 tablespoons black tea powder
- 2 cups almond milk
- ½ cup low-fat butter
- 2 cups coconut sugar
- 4 eggs
- 2 teaspoons vanilla extract
- ½ cup olive oil
- 3 and ½ cups whole wheat flour
- 1 teaspoon baking soda
- 3 teaspoons baking powder

Directions:

1. Put the milk in a pot, heat it up over medium heat, add tea, stir, take off heat and cool down.
2. Add butter, sugar, eggs, vanilla, oil, flour, baking soda and baking powder, stir well, pour into a square pan, spread, introduce in the oven, bake at 350 degrees F for 35 minutes, cool down, slice and serve. Enjoy!

Nutrition: Calories 220, Fat 4, Fiber 4, Carbs 12, Protein 7

49. Lovely Faux Mac and Cheese

Preparation time: 15 minutes

Cooking Time: 45 minutes

Serving: 4

Ingredients:

- 5 cups cauliflower florets
- Salt and pepper to taste
- 1 cup coconut milk
- ½ cup vegetable broth
- 2 tablespoons coconut flour, sifted
- 1 organic egg, beaten
- 2 cups cheddar cheese

Directions:

1. Preheat your oven to 350 degrees F.
2. Season florets with salt and steam until firm.
3. Place florets in greased ovenproof dish.
4. Heat coconut milk over medium heat in a skillet, make sure to season the oil with salt and pepper.
5. Stir in broth and add coconut flour to the mix, stir.
6. Cook until the sauce begins to bubble.
7. Remove heat and add beaten egg.
8. Pour the thick sauce over cauliflower and mix in cheese.
9. Bake for 30-45 minutes.
10. Serve and enjoy!

Nutrition: Calories: 229; Fat: 14g; Carbohydrates: 9g; Protein: 15g

50. Beautiful Banana Custard

Preparation time: 10 minutes

Cooking Time: 25 minutes

Serving: 3

Ingredients:

- 2 ripe bananas, peeled and mashed finely
- ½ teaspoon of vanilla extract
- 14-ounce unsweetened almond milk
- 3 eggs

Directions:

1. Preheat your oven to 350 degrees F.
2. Grease 8 custard glasses lightly.
3. Arrange the glasses in a large baking dish.
4. Take a large bowl and mix all of the ingredients and mix them well until combined nicely.
5. Divide the mixture evenly between the glasses.
6. Pour water in the baking dish.
7. Bake for 25 minutes.
8. Take out and serve.
9. Enjoy!

Nutrition: Calories: 59; Fat: 2.4g; Carbohydrates: 7g; Protein: 3g otein: 2g